Linking art to the world around us

Arty Facts

Space
& Art Activities

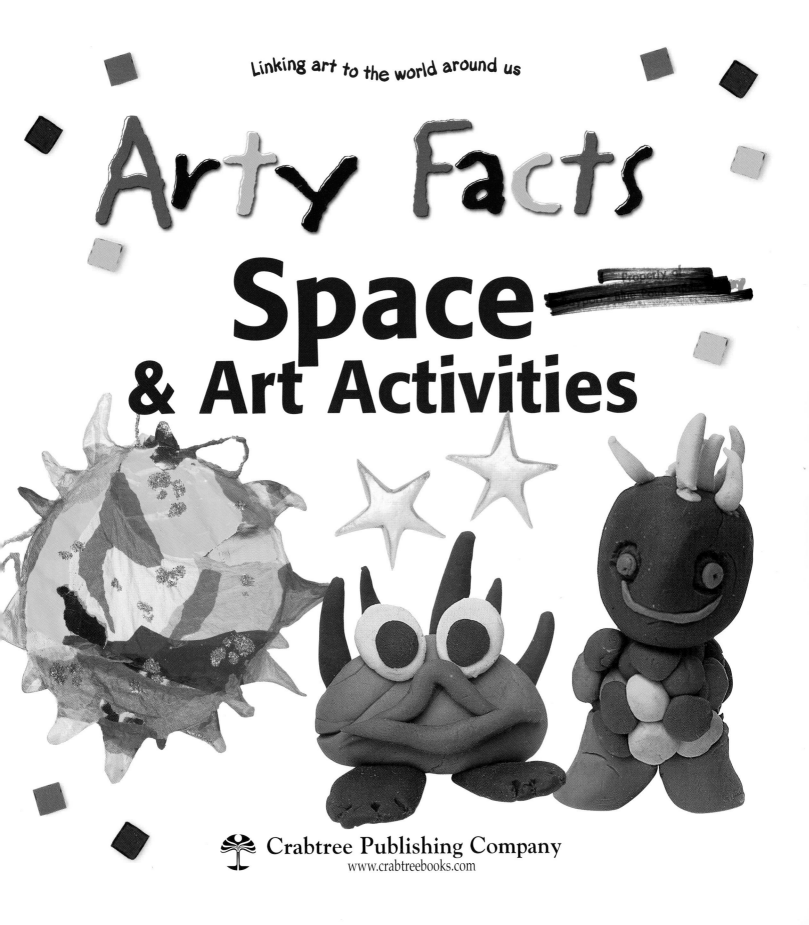

Crabtree Publishing Company
www.crabtreebooks.com

Crabtree Publishing Company

PMB 16A, 350 Fifth Avenue, Suite 3308
New York, NY
10118

612 Welland Avenue
St. Catharines, Ontario
L2M 5V6

Coordinating Editor: Ellen Rodger
Project Editors: P.A. Finlay, Carrie Gleason
Production Coordinator: Rosie Gowsell
Proofreading, Indexing: Wendy Scavuzzo

Project Development and Concept Marshall Direct:
Editorial Project Director: Karen Foster
Editors: Claire Sippi, Hazel Songhurst, Samantha Sweeney
Researchers: Gerry Bailey, Alec Edgington
Design Director: Tracy Carrington
Designers: Flora Awolaja, Claire Penny, Paul Montague,
James Thompson, Mark Dempsey,
Production: Edward MacDermott, Victoria Grimsell, Christina Brown
Photo Research: Andrea Sadler
Illustrator: Jan Smith
Model Artist: Sophie Dean

Prepress, printing and binding by Worzalla Publishing Company

Cataloging in Publication Data
Goodman, Polly.
    Space & art activities / written by Polly Goodman.
        p. cm. -- (Arty facts)
Includes index
    Summary: Information about various topics related to astronomy
forms the foundation for projects about the sun and moon, planet
rotation, space travel, black holes, and more.
    ISBN 0-7787-1140-4 (pbk.) -- ISBN 0-7787-1112-9 (rlb)
    1. Astronomy--Juvenile literature. [1. Astronomy. 2. Handicraft.]
I. Title: Space and art activities. II. Title. III. Series.
    QB46 .G69 2002
    520--dc21   2002001301
                                              LC

Created by
Marshall Direct Learning

© 2002 Marshall Direct Learning

FRONT COVER IMAGES: MAX-PLANCK-INSTITUT FUR EXTRATERRESTRISCHE PHYSIK/ SCIENCE PHOTO LIBRARY; ASTROFOTO/ BRUCE COLEMAN COLLECTION; NASA

Linking art to the world around us

Arty Facts

Space

& Art Activities

Contents

WRITTEN BY Polly Goodman

Solar system

Earth is one of nine planets in our **solar system**. The Sun is at the center of the solar system and the planets **orbit** on a circular path around it. The solar system was formed more than four billion years ago from a swirling **mass** of gas, dust, and ice. As the Sun was forming, some of the **matter** was pulled together into clumps by the force of **gravity**.

Big and small clumps

The newly formed clumps close to the Sun were mostly made of heavy rock-like matter. The Sun's powerful heat pushed away the lighter, more gaseous matter and it collected together in masses farther away.

Joined-up clumps

When the clumps joined together, they formed nine planets. Sometimes, smaller chunks of matter that did not form into either planets or moons that orbit the planets, crashed into the planets. Our own Moon is covered with craters caused by these crashes, or impacts.

Nine planets and asteroid belt

The inner planets are named Mercury, Venus, Earth, and Mars. The outer planets are called Jupiter, Saturn, Uranus, Neptune, and Pluto. There may be other planets farther out in the solar system. Between Mars and Jupiter lies the **asteroid** belt, made up of thousands of small, odd-shaped clumps of rock that slowly orbit the Sun. The asteroid belt was probably made up of clumps that did not form into full-sized planets when the solar system was born.

Space

Add spiral galaxies and sparkling discs

WHAT YOU NEED

newspaper

bucket

needle

paste

glue

paints and brush

wire

bamboo sticks

1 Tear off pieces of newspaper and soak them overnight in a bucket of water.

2 Squeeze as much water as you can from the soaked paper.

3 Make planets by dipping the paper into the paste and shaping it into several different size balls. Let them dry.

4 Paint your planets different colors.

5 Push the needle through the middle of each ball. Thread a piece of wire through the hole. Glue into place.

6 Make wire stars and different galaxy shapes to add to your mobile.

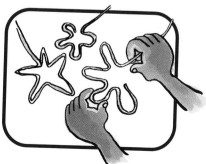

Tie two bamboo sticks together in a cross. Hang your stars, planets, and galaxies from them.

5

Blue world

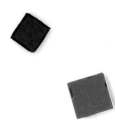

Water, land, and air

As far as we know, Earth is the only planet in the solar system where there is life. It is the only planet with liquid water on its surface and **oxygen** in its **atmosphere**. The Earth's landscapes vary from rocky mountaintops to green valleys, and from dry, barren deserts to hot, wet rainforests. At the Antarctic, the land is almost completely covered in ice. Surrounding the Earth is its atmosphere, which is a layer of **gases** that protect the Earth from the Sun's harmful rays and keeps it warm like a blanket.

Spinning globe

The Earth spins like a top as it travels around the Sun. It spins around its **axis**, an imaginary line that runs through the middle of Earth from north to south. Its spinning motion causes day and night, as each side of the Earth faces toward and then away from the Sun. It takes 365 days, or one year, for Earth to travel around the Sun. Since the Earth's axis is tilted, its movement around the Sun causes seasons to change. The northern part of Earth tilts toward the Sun in summer and away from the Sun in winter.

If you were an **astronaut** floating in space, planet Earth would look like a large blue ball with white swirls on its surface. Its blue color comes from the vast oceans that cover Earth's surface. The white swirls are clouds. You would also see the complete darkness of outer space all around the planet.

Earth's magnetic field

We live on a massive **magnet**! All around the Earth is a giant magnetic field, just like the magnetic field around a bar magnet. What makes Earth magnetic? Deep inside the Earth, there is a core of hot molten metal. Our world is always spinning, so this causes electric currents in the molten metal. These currents create the magnetic field around the Earth.

Space

Fridge magnets

WHAT YOU NEED

clay

magnets

paints and brush

glue

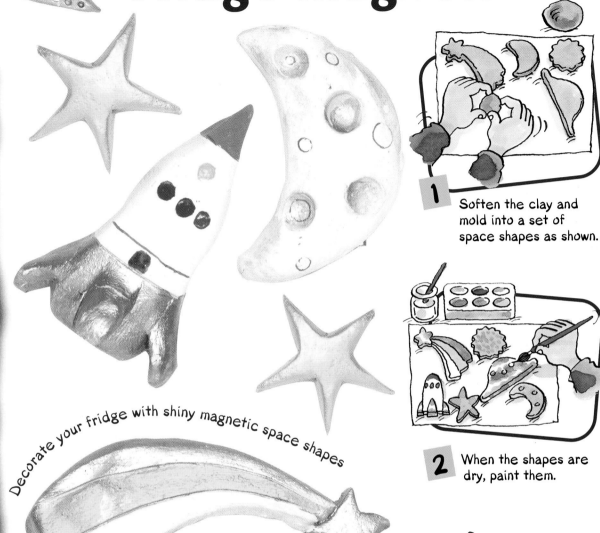

Decorate your fridge with shiny magnetic space shapes

1 Soften the clay and mold into a set of space shapes as shown.

2 When the shapes are dry, paint them.

3 Glue magnets to the backs of the space shapes.

7

Spectacular Sun

The Sun is a giant ball of burning gases, hotter than we could ever imagine. It is a **star**, like the billions of other stars in the universe, but it seems bigger than other stars because it is closer to Earth. The Sun is the most important star to Earth because it provides heat and light that are essential for life on our planet.

Light and heat energy

At the core, or center, of the Sun, the temperature is 27 million°F (15 million°C). At this temperature, the particles of gas that make up the Sun react together to make **nuclear energy**. The energy travels from the center and eventually escapes from the surface as light and heat.

Surface and atmosphere

The Sun's surface is called the photosphere. The photosphere is the source of light and heat energy.

The photosphere is surrounded by millions of miles of the Sun's atmosphere. The atmosphere is made up of two main parts: the chromosphere, a hotter inner layer, and the corona, which is the outermost layer. Throughout the atmosphere, explosions of gases, called flares, erupt. Gigantic arches of gases, called prominences, stretch from the chromosphere to the corona.

Sunspots

The surface of the Sun is speckled with dark-looking areas called sunspots. These spots occur where the Sun's magnetic field on the surface is so strong that it cools down certain areas, making them appear darker.

Solar winds

As the Sun's hot gases expand from the corona, they form solar winds that spiral outward into space. The winds extend nine billion miles (15 billion km) from the Sun, reaching speeds of up to 620 miles (1,000 km) a second. As they travel past Earth, the solar winds squeeze its magnetic field into a teardrop shape.

Space

WHAT YOU NEED

wire

tissue paper

scissors

glitter

gold paper

glue

clear and colored acetate or cellophane

gold thread

beads

Sun catcher

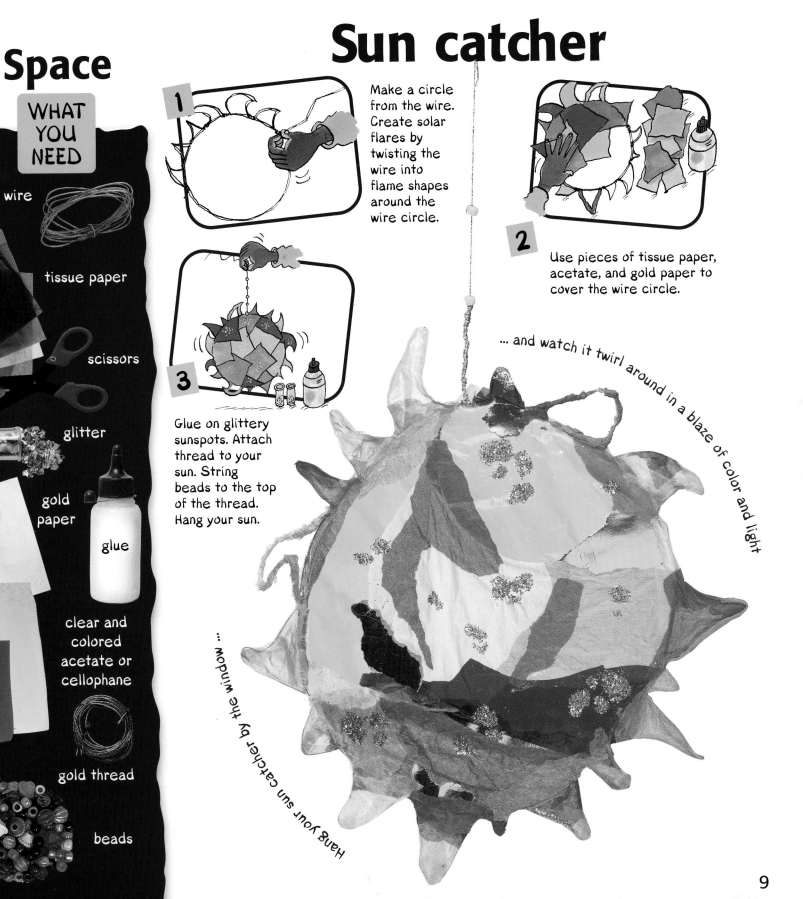

1 Make a circle from the wire. Create solar flares by twisting the wire into flame shapes around the wire circle.

2 Use pieces of tissue paper, acetate, and gold paper to cover the wire circle.

3 Glue on glittery sunspots. Attach thread to your sun. String beads to the top of the thread. Hang your sun.

Hang your sun catcher by the window ...

... and watch it twirl around in a blaze of color and light

Mysterious Moon

The stages of a lunar eclipse as the Moon passes into Earth's shadow.

The Moon is the Earth's closest neighbor. There is no life on the Moon. Pulled by the Earth's gravity, the Moon orbits, or circles, the Earth. It is the only other place in space that humans have visited.

New Moon to new Moon

The Moon has no light of its own. It shines because it reflects light from the Sun. As it rotates around the Earth, we see different parts of the Moon lit up. It takes about a month for the Moon to completely circle the Earth, so the Moon follows a cycle that is repeated every month. The cycle starts with a new Moon, when the Moon looks completely dark.

This is because it is between the Sun and the Earth, so the side facing us is in darkness. Over the next two weeks, the sunlit part of the Moon gets bigger. It becomes a crescent, a half Moon, and a full Moon. Then the pattern reverses and the sunlit part gets smaller, from full Moon to half Moon and then new Moon again.

Lunar eclipse

Once or twice a year, when the Moon should be full, it passes through Earth's shadow. The Moon's face gets darker, causing a **lunar eclipse**. In a total lunar eclipse, the whole Moon passes through the central, or darkest part of Earth's shadow. In a partial eclipse, only part of the Moon is in the center of the shadow.

10

Space

WHAT YOU NEED

black and white paint

paintbrush

black and white paper

glitter

pencil

glue

poster board

Lunar collage

Make black and white crescent moons for your bedroom wall

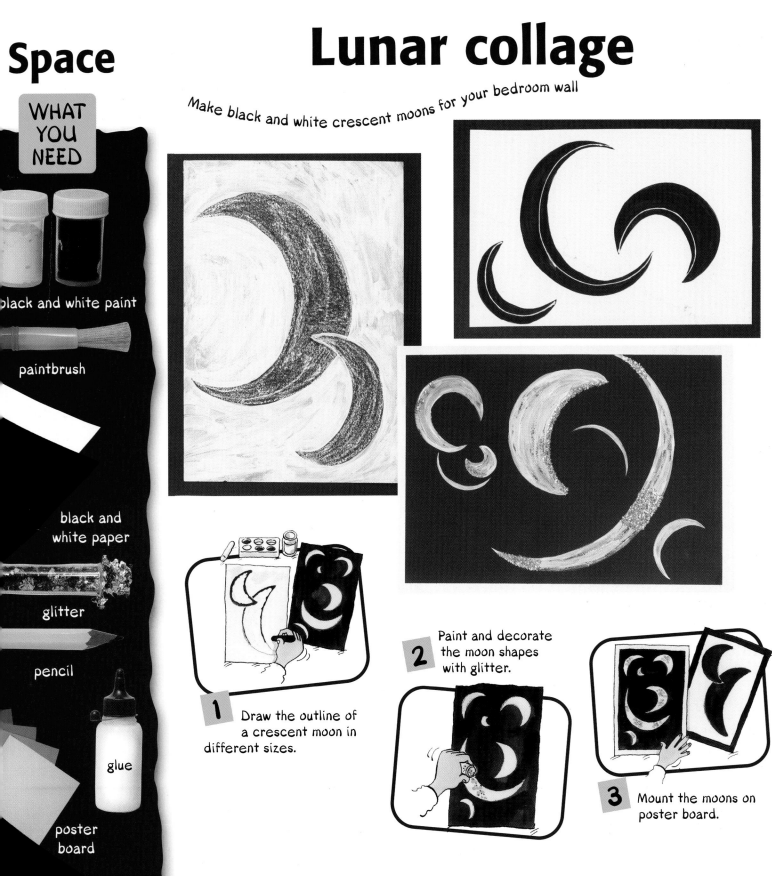

1 Draw the outline of a crescent moon in different sizes.

2 Paint and decorate the moon shapes with glitter.

3 Mount the moons on poster board.

Mighty Jupiter

Jupiter is the biggest and heaviest planet in the solar system. Through binoculars you can see four large moons that circle the planet. If you look through a telescope, you can see many different colored clouds surrounding this giant ball of gas and its faint ring of dust.

Stormy planet

A day on Jupiter lasts just 9 hours and 55 minutes compared to Earth's 24 hours, since this is the time it takes for Jupiter to spin on its axis. Its spinning speed whips up whirling winds of more than 370 miles (600 km) an hour. Storms on this mighty planet can even be seen from Earth. Jupiter's storms blow its clouds into ever-changing patterns.

Great Red Spot

For more than 300 years, a hurricane called the Great Red Spot has been spiraling in Jupiter's atmosphere. The hurricane is three times the size of Earth. It hovers five miles (8 km) above the clouds, drawing up damp air and whipping it into a spiral. When the hurricane is very strong, it looks like a deep red spot against the rest of the planet's creamy color. When it is weaker, the hurricane is more difficult to see.

Jupiter's moons

Jupiter's sixteen moons range in size from Ganymede, which is 3,273 miles (5,268 km) wide, to the tiny Leda, with a diameter of only 6.2 miles (10 km).

A close-up view of Jupiter's Great Red Spot.

Stripey ball

WHAT YOU NEED

balloon

newspaper

glue

paints and brush

small tin tart plate

gold thread

glass beads

beads

scissors

sequins

1 
Blow up the balloon. Glue strips of newspaper on the balloon, building up several layers. Leave it to dry.

Paint and splatter on yellow, orange, and red colors for a stripey, marbled effect.

2

3 
Flatten the tin tart plate and glue glass beads and sequins to it.

4 
Pop and throw away the balloon. Decorate a piece of gold thread with beads and sequins. Attach the thread to the top of your model.

Hang your Jupiter mobile from the ceiling and admire its red spot

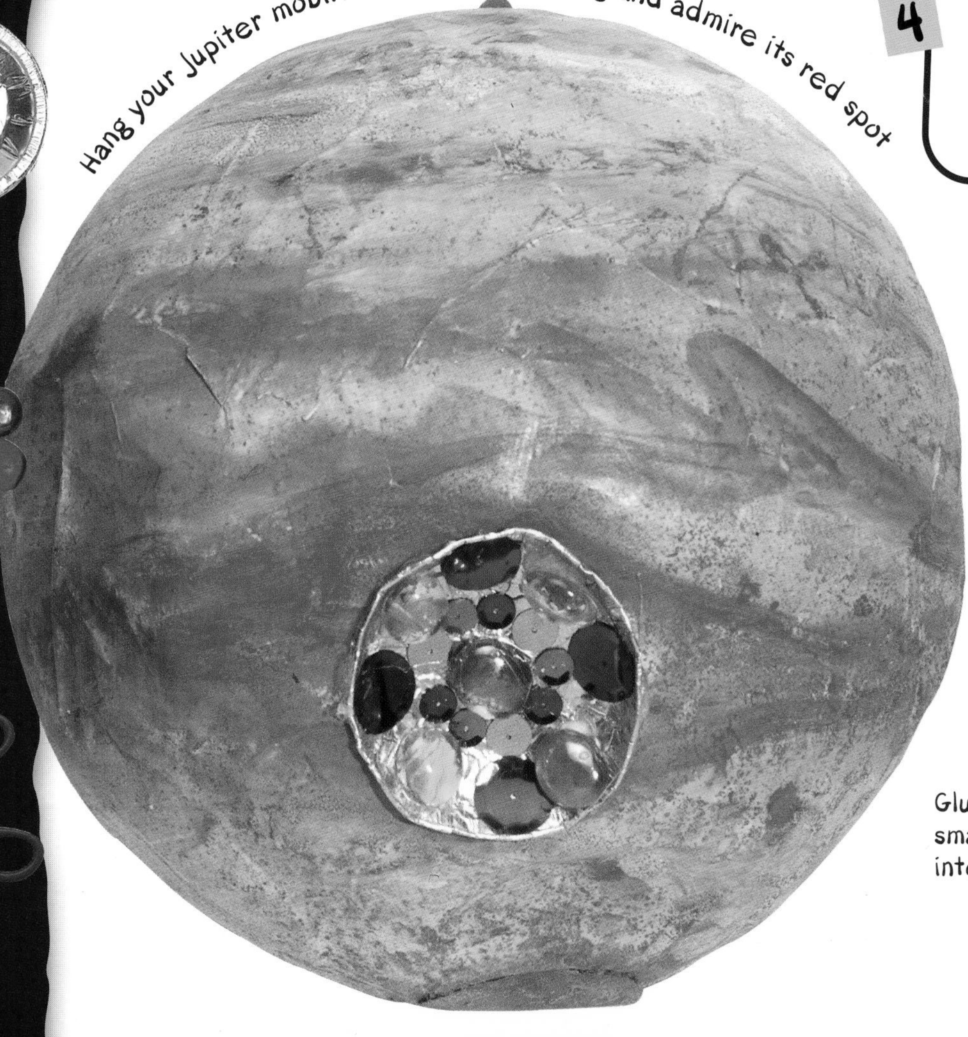

Glue the decorated small tin tart plate into place.

13

Starry patterns

On a clear night, the sky twinkles with thousands of stars. One way to find your way around the night sky is by looking for a familiar bright star and then locating other stars from it. Up to 2,500 stars are visible with the human eye. With binoculars and a telescope, you can see as many as 6,000 stars.

Constellations

Constellations are patterns made by the stars. Star maps show the shapes of constellations by joining a group of stars with lines, like connecting dots. The ancient Arabs, Greeks, and Romans named many constellations after animals or figures they saw in the patterns. The Pleiades were named after seven sisters in an ancient Greek myth.

Brightest star

In the northern hemisphere, one of the easiest constellations to find is the Little Dipper. It is visible all year round. Look for a saucepan shape made up of seven stars. The edge of the saucepan points toward the North Star, or Pole Star, which is in almost exactly the same position every night, above the North Pole. The brightest star in the northern hemisphere is Arcturus, which is part of a constellation called the Herdsman. The brightest star of all is Sirius, or the Dog Star. Sirius can only be seen from the southern hemisphere. It is part of a constellation called Canis Major. In the southern hemisphere, the Southern Cross is the brightest star in the night sky.

The Pleiades constellation.

Space

WHAT YOU NEED

- black poster board
- scissors
- toothbrush
- glitter
- gold thread
- metallic paints
- brush
- glue
- white poster board
- glitter glue
- shiny paper

Create a night sky and fill it with amazing stars

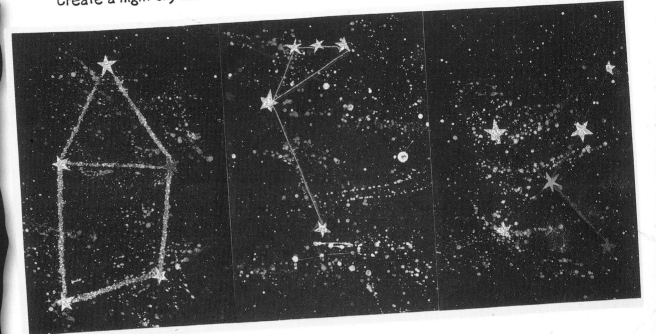

1 Use the paint and toothbrush to splatter patterns on the black poster board.

2 Cut stars from the shiny paper and glue them to the black poster board in constellation shapes.

3 Join the shiny stars together with glitter glue and gold thread.

4 Mount the black poster board onto white poster board.

15

The red planet

Mars is one of Earth's closest neighbors. It is red because of the iron in its soil and rocks. When winds blow up red dust from the ground, they create skies the color of strawberries. Mars was named after the Roman god of war, because red is a color of blood, anger, and warfare.

Life on Mars

For more than 300 years, people have been wondering if there is life on Mars. More than any other planet in our solar system, the surface of Mars closely resembles that of Earth. It has clouds, weather, and an atmosphere. In 1965, when the space probe Mariner 4 sent back photographs of Mars's surface, hopes of life on the planet were dashed. The photographs showed no signs of life, with no surface water. Scientists believe that Mars had surface water in the past and that it may now be frozen under ice. In 1996, a **meteorite** was discovered that fell from Mars onto Antarctica thousands of years ago. The meteorite contained **fossils** of bacteria and other evidence of living organisms on Mars. It is possible that there was once life on Mars a very long time ago. Many scientists believe it is unlikely that life still exists on the planet.

Mars visitor

In 1997, the Pathfinder spacecraft landed on Mars. It used a six-wheeled vehicle called the Sojourner Rover to explore Mars and test the soil and atmosphere. Scientists used radio control from Earth to direct Sojourner on Mars.

Space base

Scientists believe Mars is a perfect base for future space exploration because it is similar to Earth. Studies of Mars's climate could be used to understand Earth's climate and the search for life on Mars. The planet could be made **habitable** by releasing **carbon dioxide** in the ice caps.

Space

WHAT YOU NEED

white poster board

paints and brush

pastels

glue

colored construction paper

Martian art

1 Draw circles of different sizes and colors on construction paper. Mix the pastel colors as you draw.

2 Paint circles of different sizes and colors on another piece of construction paper.

3 Glue the circles on white poster board.

Can you draw smooth round circles?

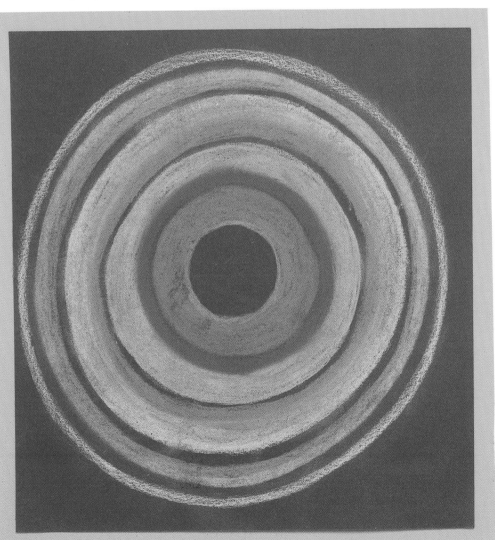

Dust clouds

Some of the most spectacular pictures from space show colorful clouds of glowing dust and gases. These dust clouds are often too faint to see with the human eye.

Even with a telescope, dust clouds appear as small, pale smoke rings and smudges. Special cameras are able to pick up their colors and shapes.

What are nebulae?

Nebulae are clouds of dust and gases. Their name comes from the Latin word for clouds. Most scientists believe that our whole solar system was formed from one giant spiralling nebula. There are two main types of nebulae: planetary nebulae and diffuse nebulae.

Planetary nebulae

When a star dies, it throws off its outer layers, that then form into glowing clouds of gas and dust. These clouds are called planetary nebulae.

Hot and cold stars

Diffuse nebulae are bigger than planetary nebulae. **Astronomers** have divided diffuse nebulae into three different types: emission, reflection, and dark nebulae. Emission, or glowing, nebulae form near an extremely hot star. The star gives off so much **ultraviolet light** that gases in the cloud are heated up and glow. Reflection nebulae form when a cloud is near a cool star. The star is not hot enough to heat the gases in the cloud, but its light is reflected off dust in the cloud. These nebulae are bluish in color. Dark nebulae are dark smudges against brighter clouds. They form where there are no stars nearby to reflect their light, or where the cloud blocks out light from stars behind it.

Different gases in this nebula glow in amazing colors.

Space

WHAT YOU NEED

black construction paper

poster board

glue

sequins

silver and white paint

toothbrush

pastels

Smudge art

1 Dip the toothbrush in white and silver paint and make spots on the black construction paper.

Paint two night skies lit up by glowing stars and bright pastel dust clouds

2 Use pastels and smudge the colors so they blend together.

3 Glue on some sequins.

4 Glue your pictures on poster board.

19

Floating in space

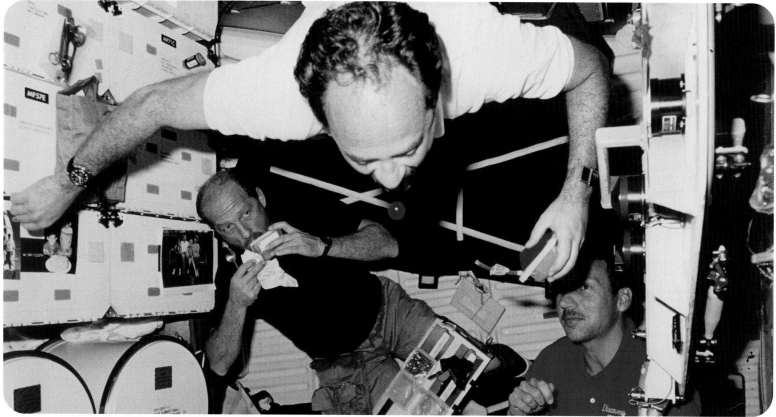

Imagine eating a cookie and the crumbs float away in the air! That is just one of the situations that astronauts face in space, where there is no oxygen, water, or gravity. Breathing, eating, drinking, and sleeping are very different experiences on a **space station**.

Getting around

The biggest problem astronauts have to overcome is the lack of gravity in a space station. Without gravity, objects do not stay where they are placed and things float around unless they are attached. When astronauts walk in space, they must use footholds, handholds, and special straps attached to walkways.

Space food

Astronauts eat pre-cooked meals that are freeze-dried, then heated. Bite-size pieces of food are covered with gelatin to stop them from floating away. Drinks do not stay in the cup, so astronauts have to drink with a straw from plastic packs.

Breathing and sleeping

Since there is no air in space, filters and fans supply the station with oxygen and remove carbon dioxide exhaled by the crew. Astronauts wear belts attached to their beds to stop them from floating around the space station when they are asleep. Space station toilets use air currents to suck waste away from astronauts' bodies and out through waste pipes.

Space

Space station

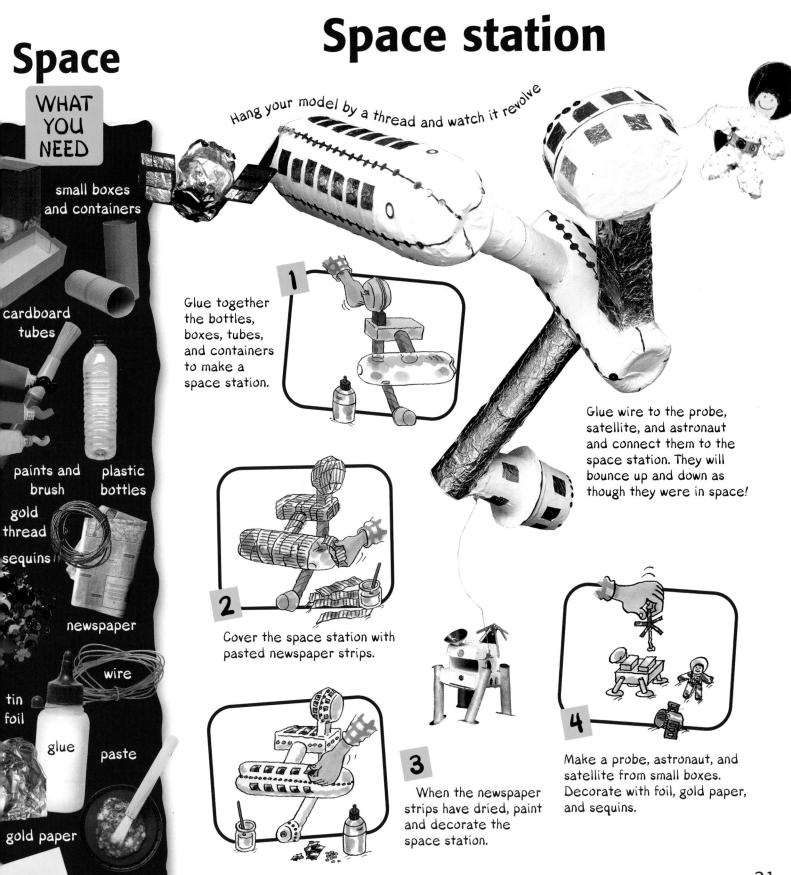

WHAT YOU NEED

- small boxes and containers
- cardboard tubes
- paints and brush
- plastic bottles
- gold thread
- sequins
- newspaper
- wire
- tin foil
- glue
- paste
- gold paper

1 Glue together the bottles, boxes, tubes, and containers to make a space station.

2 Cover the space station with pasted newspaper strips.

3 When the newspaper strips have dried, paint and decorate the space station.

4 Make a probe, astronaut, and satellite from small boxes. Decorate with foil, gold paper, and sequins.

Glue wire to the probe, satellite, and astronaut and connect them to the space station. They will bounce up and down as though they were in space!

21

Saturn's rings

Saturn is one of the most beautiful planets in the solar system. From Earth, to the human eye, it looks like a simple yellow star, but through a telescope you can see a spectacular set of rings circling its equator. Beneath the rings is Saturn's atmosphere – layers of orange and yellow clouds covered with a creamy-colored haze.

Saturn's spin

Saturn is the sixth planet from the Sun, almost ten times farther away from the Sun than Earth is. It takes almost 30 years for Saturn to travel once around the Sun, compared to the Earth's single year. A day on Saturn is much shorter than a day on Earth. It takes just 10 hours and 39 minutes for Saturn to complete one rotation compared to Earth's 24 hours.

Liquid planet

Saturn is the second largest planet in the solar system. It is a giant ball of gas and liquid, covered with colorful bands of clouds.

Rings and ringlets

Saturn has seven main rings, but each one is made up of thousands of tightly packed rings. The rings are made from billions of glittering icy fragments, ranging in size from giant icebergs to tiny particles of ice. Scientists think that long ago, **comets** caught by Saturn's gravity collided and broke into pieces, forming the rings. The rings are so thin and flat, that whenever they are in line with Earth, they are invisible.

A close-up view of Saturn's spectacular rings.

Space

Spangled bangles

scissors

sequins

beads

glue

wire

1 Make four to five semi-circles, large enough to fit around your wrist, from the wire.

2 Thread and glue a row of beads and sequins onto each wire.

Tie your beaded bracelet around your wrist

3 Twist a piece of wire around the ends of the beaded strands, so there is a knot at each end.

4 Make a loop at one end and a hook at the other end to form a clasp.

23

A star is born

On a clear night, when there are no clouds, it is possible to see up to 2,500 stars in the sky. The Sun is our nearest star, so it looks like a large glowing ball. Some stars are much bigger than the Sun, but they are so far away that they look like pin-sized specks of light.

Star birth

A new star begins as a cloud of **hydrogen**, **helium**, and dust. Over millions of years, gravity pulls these gases together into a ball. Nuclear energy is produced in the center of the ball, heating the cloud around it and making it glow. A new star is born.

Dying stars

The bigger a star, the quicker it burns up its hydrogen and the shorter its life. As the hydrogen starts to run out, a star gets much bigger. Stars that have a mass about the same as, or less than, the Sun, gradually shed their outer layers. Only the core of the star remains. The remaining white star is known as a **white dwarf**. It gradually cools, becoming dimmer and reddening, until it completely fades away. Stars that are about five times the Sun's mass, and bigger, expand and become **giants** or **supergiants**. Some supergiants are a thousand times bigger than the Sun. Giants and supergiants eventually blow up in a massive explosion called a **supernova**, leaving behind either a **neutron star** or a **black hole**.

Space

WHAT YOU NEED

- poster board
- glue
- black and white construction paper
- scissors
- paper fastener
- brush
- glitter
- silver paint
- pastels
- ruler
- pencil
- sequins

Stargazer

1 Draw and cut out a giant star from poster board. Paint it silver and decorate it with sequins and glitter.

2 Draw and cut out two circles, one white and one black.

3 Divide the black circle into six equal parts. In each part, use pastels to draw the stages in the life of a star. Glue the circle to the center of the star.

4 Paint and decorate the white circle to match the silver star. Cut out a window to show one of your pastel drawings.

5 Attach the silver circle to the black one in the middle, using a paper fastener.

Turn the disk to see the life of a star in pastel pictures

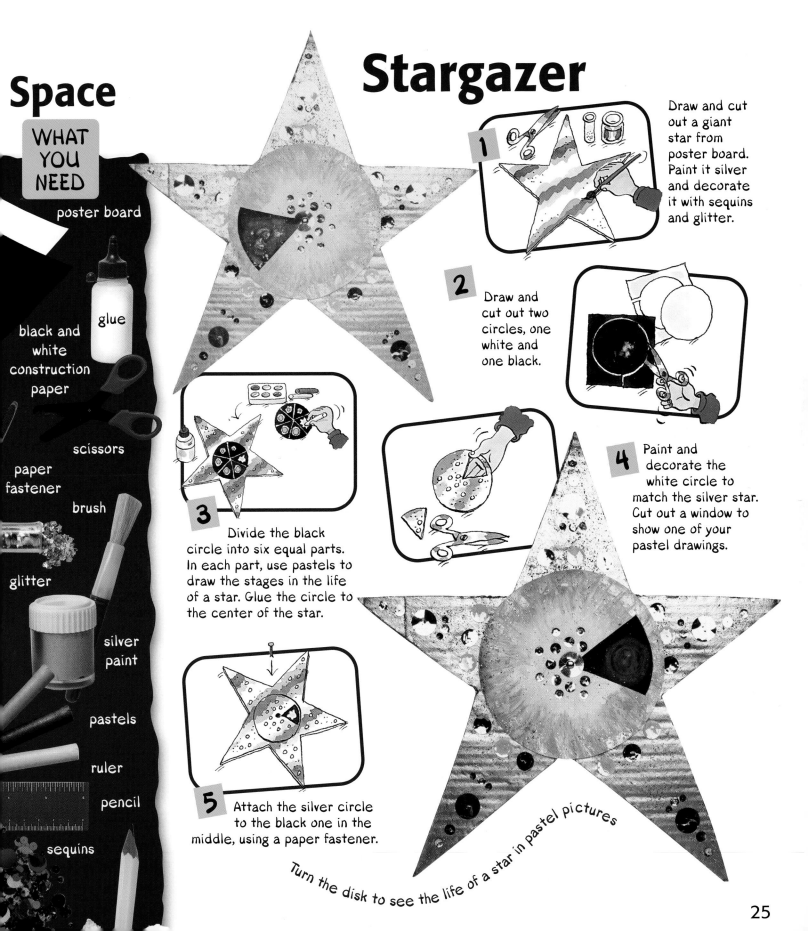

Galactic swirls

The universe is filled with many different **galaxies**. A galaxy is a system of stars, gas, and dust held together by gravity. There are billions of galaxies in the universe. Astronomers do not know exactly how many galaxies exist. There are two main types of galaxies, spiral galaxies and elliptical galaxies, named after their shape and appearance.

Active galaxies

Some galaxies have more activity going on in their centers. These are called active galaxies. Some active galaxies produce unusually strong **radio waves**. These are known as radio galaxies. **Quasars** are another kind of active galaxy. They are the most distant objects astronomers know about. They look like stars, but are about 10,000 times brighter than a normal galaxy.

Jets of gas

The nearest radio galaxy to Earth is Centaurus A. It can be seen through binoculars as a tiny blob in the sky. A radio telescope shows it has large jets of gas, called lobes, at either end of it. The jets give off light, radio waves, and **X-rays**.

Black holes

When a massive star collapses at the end of its life, a black hole forms. Astronomers believe that at the center of an active galaxy there is a giant black hole. As stars and other space debris fall toward the black hole, they form a hot swirling disc around the hole. The heat causes gas to flow off the disk in jets.

Space

Spheres and spirals

WHAT YOU NEED

glue

paints and brush

glitter glue

black construction paper

sequins

wire

gold paint

silver poster board

white pencil crayon

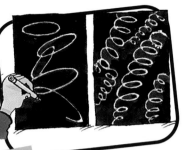

1 On a piece of black construction paper draw several spheres with a white pencil. On another piece of black paper draw spirals.

2 Paint, then decorate with gold paint, glitter glue, and sequins. Add some wire shapes.

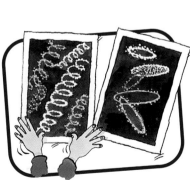

3 Mount on silver poster board.

Wire shapes will give your galactic art a 3-D look

Terrific telescopes

Telescopes help make the night sky the greatest show on Earth. We do not need telescopes to see the Moon, planets, and thousands of stars, but they help us to see much more. Without them, we would not know much about the universe. Telescopes range in size from small hand-held binoculars to large **observatories** like the Very Large Telescope in Chile, that has mirrors the size of tennis courts.

How do telescopes work?

Telescopes let us see more clearly objects that are too far away to see with the human eye. They can magnify faint stars and galaxies up to a million times by gathering and focusing light from the sky. Telescopes use a curved mirror or **lens** to collect light. The larger the lens or mirror, the more light a telescope can collect.

The more light a telescope gathers, the more information it can produce. Each of the four giant telescopes that make up the Very Large Telescope is a billion times more powerful than the human eye.

Traveling telescope

The Hubble Space Telescope is a telescope that orbits the Earth. It sits in an unmanned observatory about 373 miles (600 km) above the Earth's surface, with each orbit taking an hour and a half to complete. Hubble was launched in 1990. Its position above Earth's atmosphere means it escapes the blurring effect of the atmosphere, so it can produce much clearer images than telescopes on Earth. Hubble's main mirror measures eight feet (2.4 m) in diameter. Its power comes from solar panels, which turn sunlight into electricity. Astronomers on the ground operate the telescope by remote control, collecting its data by using radio signals.

The Hubble Space Telescope.

Space

Observatory

paints and brush

plastic bottle

glue

box lid

scissors

newspaper

acetate

poster board and cardboard

wire mesh

fabric

paste

1 Cut the plastic bottle in half. Turn the bottom half upside down. Glue on strips of newspaper.

2 Cut a triangular opening in the end of the bottle. Now paint and decorate your observatory.

3 Cut one end off a box lid and cut diagonally along the sides, so that the box lid stands up. Paint a night sky scene on it. Glue fabric on a piece of cardboard and paint a ground scene on it.

4 Roll a piece of poster board to form the telescope. Glue a piece of acetate over one end. Wedge it inside the opening of the observatory.

5 Glue the observatory to the ground cardboard. Place the sky background behind it. Attach a triangular piece of wire mesh, so it covers half of the telescope opening.

Use metallic paints to decorate your observatory for a night-time shimmer

Poison planet

Venus is one of the planets in our solar system and one of five planets we can see without a telescope. At certain times of the year, it is the first star to appear at night. Venus is about the same size as Earth. It takes Venus 225 Earth days to orbit the Sun. It is the only planet that rotates in the opposite direction to its orbit.

Venus in orbit

After Mercury, Venus is the second closest planet to the Sun. Its average distance from the Sun is about 67 million miles (108 million km). Venus sometimes passes within 26 million miles (42 million km) of Earth – closer than any other planet.

Acid atmosphere

Venus is covered by thick clouds of sulphur and sulphuric acid. **Space probes** from Earth have explored the planet's surface. Venus is hot and dry, with mountains, canyons, valleys, and flat plains. Two of the mountain ranges are bigger than any on Earth. Some areas are covered by a fine layer of dust. Other areas are littered with sharp rocks and there may be some active volcanoes.

Waterless world

There is no moisture on the surface of Venus. The planet is so hot that any water would immediately boil away. The atmosphere is mostly made up of carbon dioxide, **nitrogen** gases, and some water vapor. The **pressure** of the atmosphere, caused by the weight of these gases, is about 90 times heavier than on Earth. This heavy "air" on Venus would squash a human. Life as we know it could not exist there because of the intense heat and lack of oxygen.

Passing spacecraft

On December 15, 1970, the Soviet spacecraft Venera 7 landed on Venus. Since then, more landings have sent back photographs of its atmosphere and surface.

Space

WHAT YOU NEED

wire

string

colored tissue paper

paste

brush

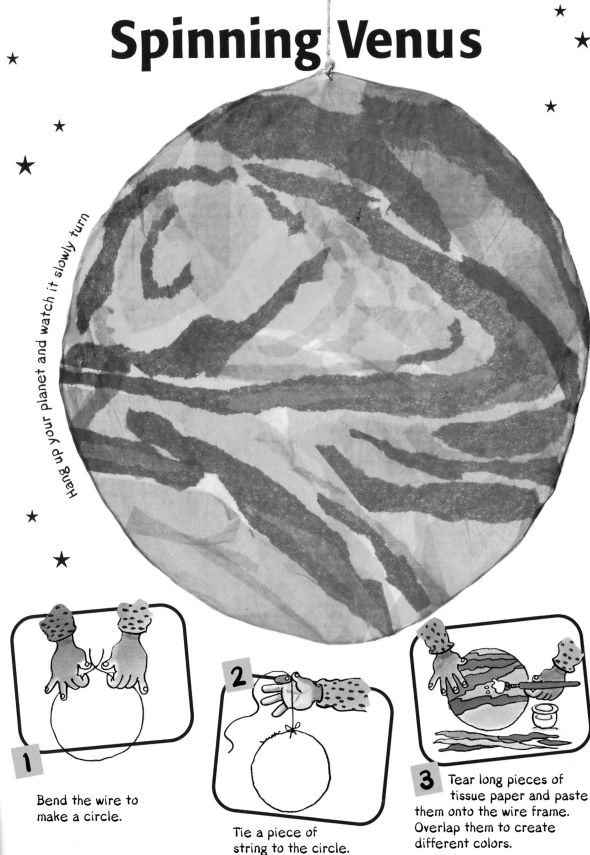

Hang up your planet and watch it slowly turn

1 Bend the wire to make a circle.

2 Tie a piece of string to the circle.

3 Tear long pieces of tissue paper and paste them onto the wire frame. Overlap them to create different colors.

31

Rocks in space

Asteroid belt

Most asteroids travel in a region called the asteroid belt, which is between 158 million miles (254 million km) and 371 million miles (598 million km) away from the Sun. Asteroids orbit the Sun in the same direction as the planets, taking three to six years for each orbit. Ceres is the biggest asteroid and was the first asteroid to be discovered. It was found in 1801. Since then, more than 9,000 asteroids have been closely studied, but scientists estimate there are more than 50,000 in total.

Collision

Scientists think that asteroids were formed billions of years ago from large balls of rock, called **protoplanets**, each about the size of the Moon. When the protoplanets collided, they broke up into smaller pieces - the asteroids. Most asteroids are thousands of miles apart, but they still collide today. If an asteroid is smaller than the one it hits, the collision makes a crater in the larger asteroid. If it is bigger, the smaller asteroid often breaks up and forms new, even smaller asteroids.

Circling the Sun between Mars and Jupiter are thousands of rocky objects called asteroids. These space rocks are also called minor planets because they spin around as they travel, just like planets. Many of the asteroids are no more than a few feet wide, but about a billion of them measure more than a half mile.

Space

WHAT YOU NEED

old belt

silver paint

small cardboard boxes

glue

sequins

small tin tart plate

glass beads

paints and brush

tin foil

toothpicks

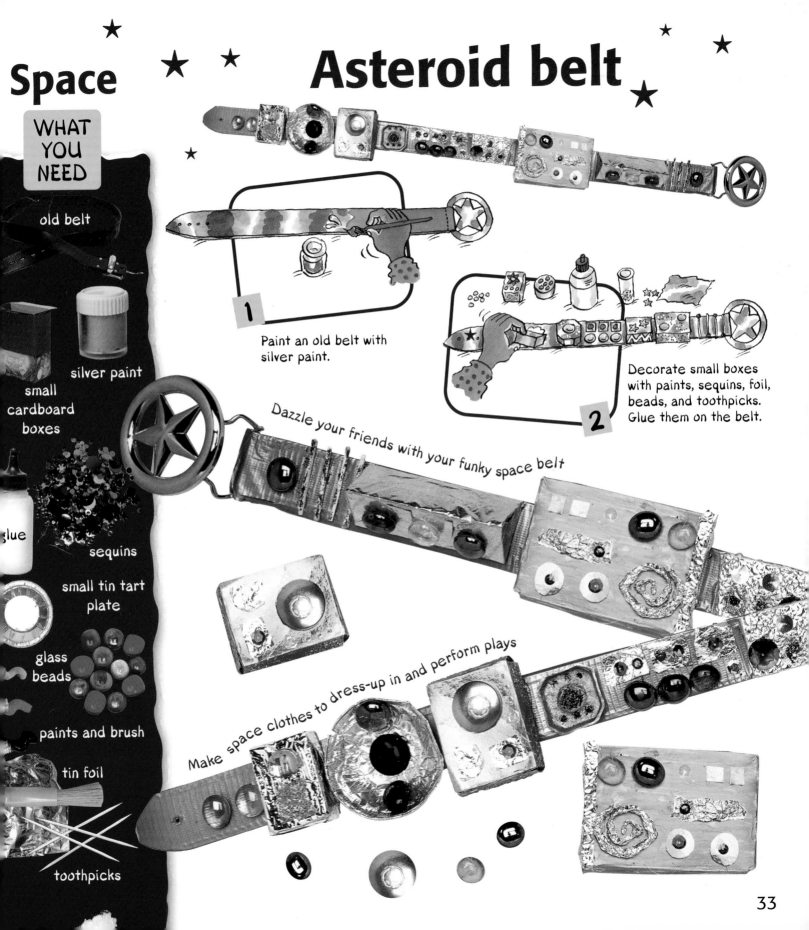

1 Paint an old belt with silver paint.

2 Decorate small boxes with paints, sequins, foil, beads, and toothpicks. Glue them on the belt.

Dazzle your friends with your funky space belt

Make space clothes to dress-up in and perform plays

Spinning top

Mercury is the closest planet to the Sun, and the second smallest in the solar system after Pluto. Mercury is dry and rocky, with a cratered surface caused by meteorites. Mercury is so close to the Sun that you can only see it at certain times of the year. It looks like a bright star and is best seen near the horizon, either in the west just after sunset, or in the east just before sunrise.

Swift Mercury

Since it is so close to the Sun, Mercury is the fastest planet to travel around it, traveling at 30 miles (48 km) a second. It takes just 88 days for Mercury to complete one orbit of the Sun, compared to Earth's 365 days. It might be quick to orbit the Sun, but Mercury spins slowly on its axis. A day on Mercury lasts the equivalent of 176 days on Earth.

Scorched earth

The Sun scorches Mercury's surface to incredibly high temperatures. The Sun's rays are seven times stronger on Mercury than they are on Earth, and the planet has so little atmosphere that there is little protection from the heat. Daytime temperatures can soar to over 800°F (427°C), while at night they can drop to under -279°F (−173°C).

Craggy planet

Mercury's surface is pockmarked with craters and scarred by ridges and crags. The craters are from the impact of meteorites that crashed into it billions of years ago. The Caloris Basin is large, with a central crater more than 800 miles (1,300 km) wide, surrounded by several rings of mountains that cover about 2,287 miles (3,680 km).

Space

Mercury maze game

WHAT YOU NEED

poster board and cardboard

pencil

metallic paints

brush

black paint

glue

sequins

marbles

tin foil

scissors

red paper

1 Draw a large circle onto a piece of cardboard. Cut out and paint a night sky on it. Glue on sequins.

2 Cut strips of poster board and cover them with tin foil.

3 Glue the strips onto the circle from the outside in. Leave gaps for the marbles to pass through.

4 Cut a circle from red paper to make a bull's-eye. Cut four holes big enough to hold the marbles. Glue into the middle of the board.

Move your marbles through the space maze and get all four to Mercury's bull's-eye!

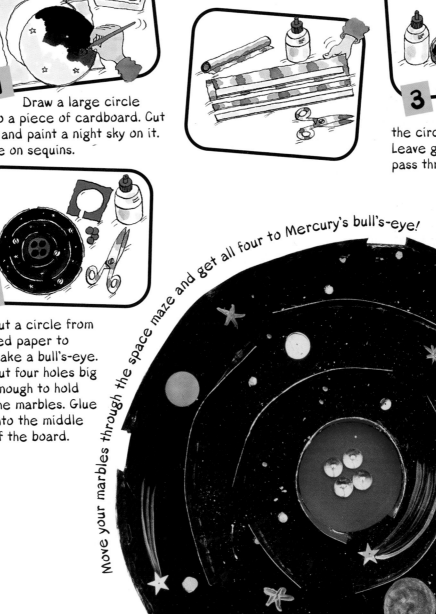

35

Space walking

Imagine a place with no air, with temperatures that vary from extreme hot to extreme cold, and where particles of dust travel at speeds that could kill you. These are just some of the situations astronauts have to cope with when they travel in space. The strangest condition is the lack of gravity.

Coping without gravity

Gravity is a force that makes objects move toward each other. The Earth's gravity keeps your feet on the ground and makes objects fall down by pulling them toward Earth. On a spaceship, there is no gravity and everything floats in the air. It takes a while for an astronaut's body to get used to living in space and many astronauts suffer space sickness for the first few days or weeks.

Steps in space

When astronauts leave the spaceship, they have to wear a space suit that lets them breathe and protects them from heat, cold, and space debris. A backpack linked to the helmet supplies oxygen and takes away carbon dioxide and moisture. The space suit has a radio, so the astronaut can communicate with others inside the spaceship and with ground control back on Earth. The front of the helmet blocks out harmful rays from the Sun. When working on the outside of a space station, a lifeline attaches the space suit to the station to stop the astronaut from floating away.

Space

WHAT YOU NEED

egg carton

cardboard boxes

glue

wire

paints and brush

tin foil

sequins

black pen

fabric

poster board

black paper

Cutaway capsule

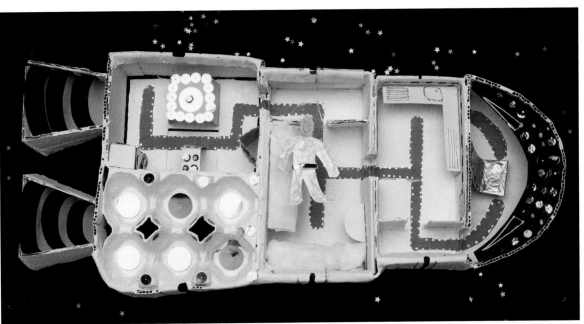

Mount your spaceship against a starry sky

1

Glue different-sized boxes together to make the space capsule.

2 Make rocket engines from cardboard and glue on strips of black paper. Glue the engines to the capsule. Paint the whole model.

3

Make each compartment different. Use black paper and sequins to make a bridge in the control room. Glue a commander's foil chair inside.

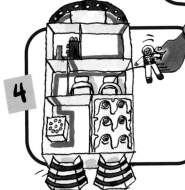

4

Make beds from fabric and glue them into the compartment. Connect an astronaut to the bed with wire.

37

Distant planets

Thick blue clouds cover the planet Neptune.

Blue planets

Uranus and Neptune are known as the blue planets because they are covered in thick blue clouds. The blue color comes from the gas called methane that exists in their atmospheres. Both Uranus and Neptune are mainly made of water, along with methane and ammonia gases. They both have rings surrounding their equators and a family of moons. Uranus has at least seventeen known moons and Neptune has at least eight.

Seasons and storms

Uranus has eleven rings around its equator. Ten of them are black and narrow. Uranus rotates on its side as it orbits the Sun. This means it has long seasons, with each pole in total darkness for 42 years, followed by 42 years of light when the Sun never sets. Neptune has four faint rings of dust. Its atmosphere is struck by violent storms, with winds blowing at about 1,243 miles (2,000 km) an hour.

Ice dwarf

Pluto is the smallest planet in the solar system, with only one moon. Most of the time, Pluto is the farthest planet from the Sun. Every 248 years, Pluto's orbit takes it closer to the Sun than Neptune, where it stays for about 20 years. When it is nearer to the Sun, Pluto's icy surface turns to gas. When it is farther away from the Sun, Pluto becomes completely frozen again.

Far out at the edges of the solar system are the distant giant planets, Uranus and Neptune. They are both about four times the size of Earth. Beyond them, sitting on the very rim of the solar system, is the tiny planet Pluto. Scientists think that Pluto may be one of millions of small, icy worlds that orbit the Sun beyond Neptune, in a region known as the Kuiper Belt.

Space

stick

glue

paints and brush

poster board

pencil

scissors

glitter

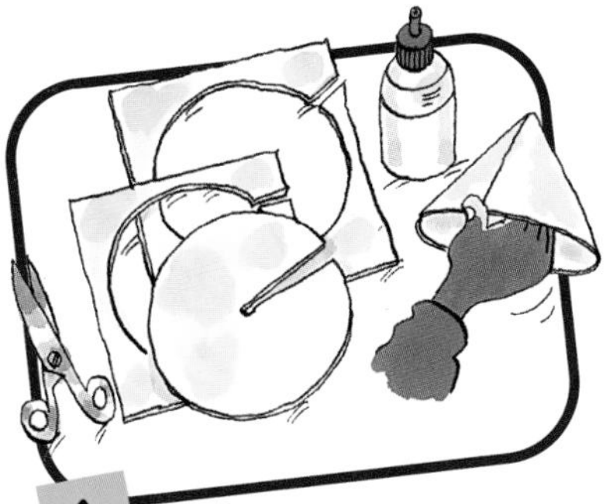

Spinning top

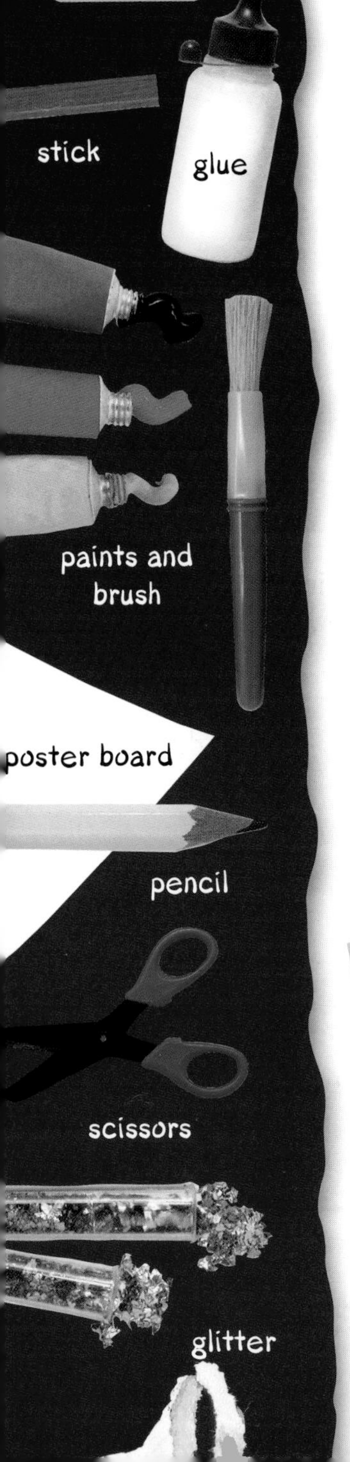

1 Draw and cut out two circles from poster board. Make a cut from the rim to the center of each circle to form cones. Leave a small opening at the ends.

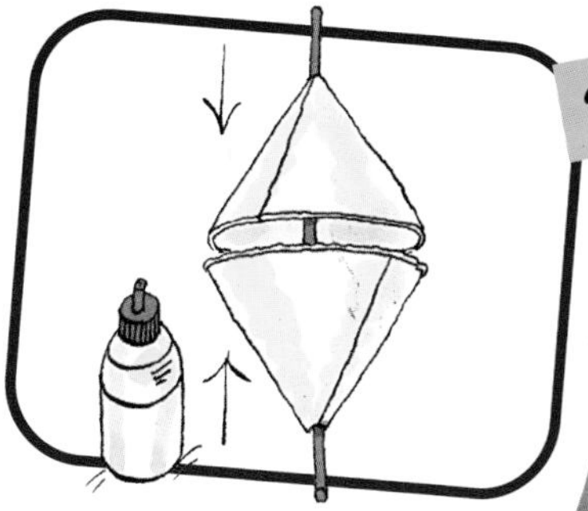

2 Poke a stick through the holes of both cones and glue the cones together in the middle.

3 Paint and decorate the bottom half with icy colors and the top with hot colors.

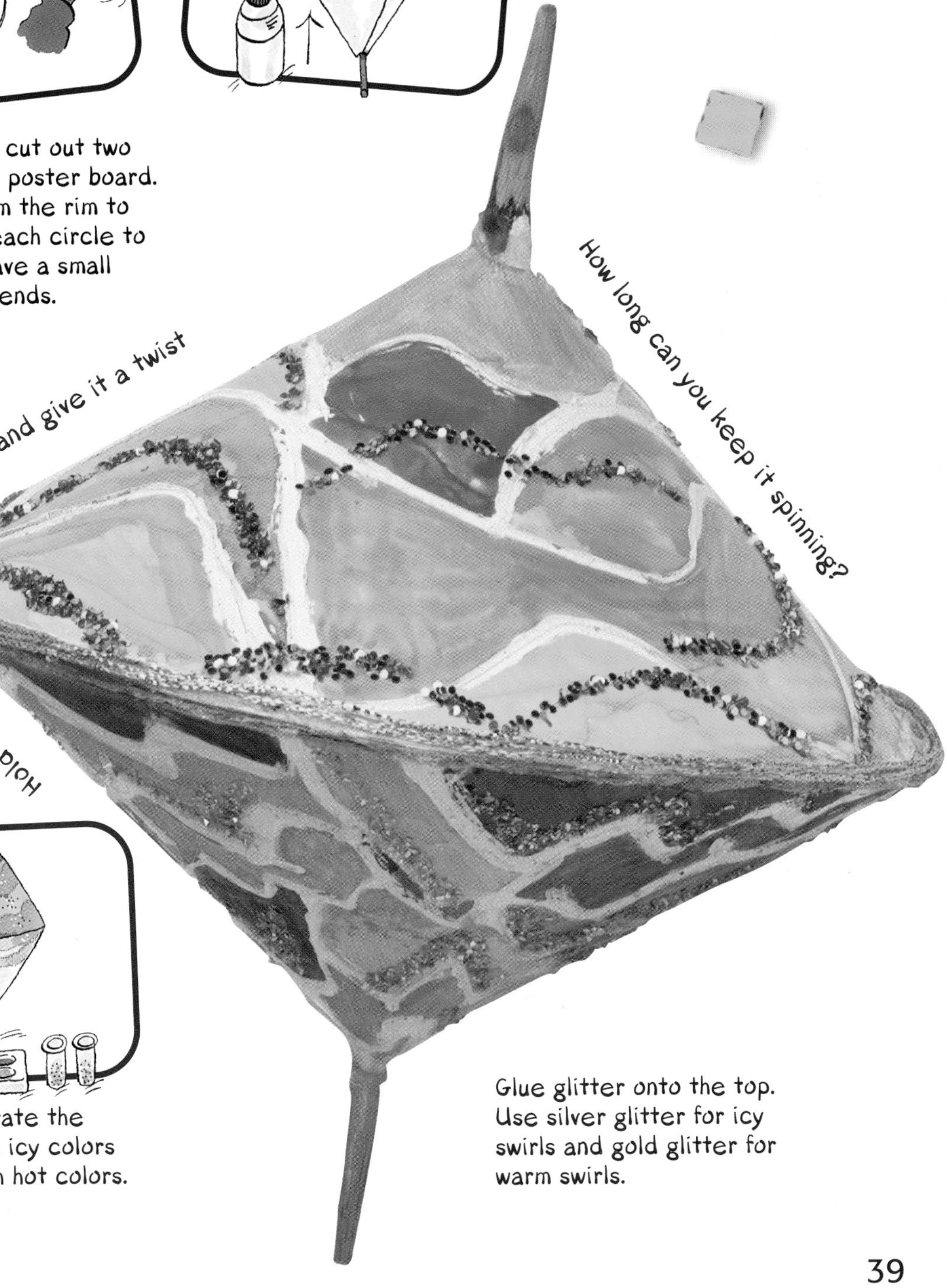

Hold the top upright on a flat surface and give it a twist

How long can you keep it spinning?

Glue glitter onto the top. Use silver glitter for icy swirls and gold glitter for warm swirls.

Trails of light

Every night, bright streaks of light move across the Earth's skies. These are called **meteors**, or shooting stars, but they are not stars at all. Meteors occur when fragments of rock enter the Earth's atmosphere. When the fragments, called **meteoroids**, enter the Earth's atmosphere, they cause a lot of friction as they push through the air. This makes them so hot that they burn up, leaving behind a bright trail of light.

Comets

Comets are giant lumps of snow and dust, like dirty snowballs, that orbit the Sun. When comets travel close to the Sun, the Sun's heat and wind changes their shape. They form a hot, glowing head and two tails. The tails can be more than 62 million miles (100 million km) long. Most comets are a long way from the Sun and the planets, at the edge of the solar system, but sometimes they travel closer. This is when we see them in the sky. Certain comets appear often in the sky. A beautiful comet called Hale-Bopp was last seen in 1997 and will return in about 2007.

Crash landing

Meteoroids that survive the Earth's atmosphere and reach the ground are called meteorites. About 3,000 meteorites land on the Earth each year. Most are small pieces of rock, but if they are very big, they crash into the ground. The impact causes an explosion, forming a crater in the ground.

The Hale-Bopp comet streaks across the sky.

Space

Shooting comet

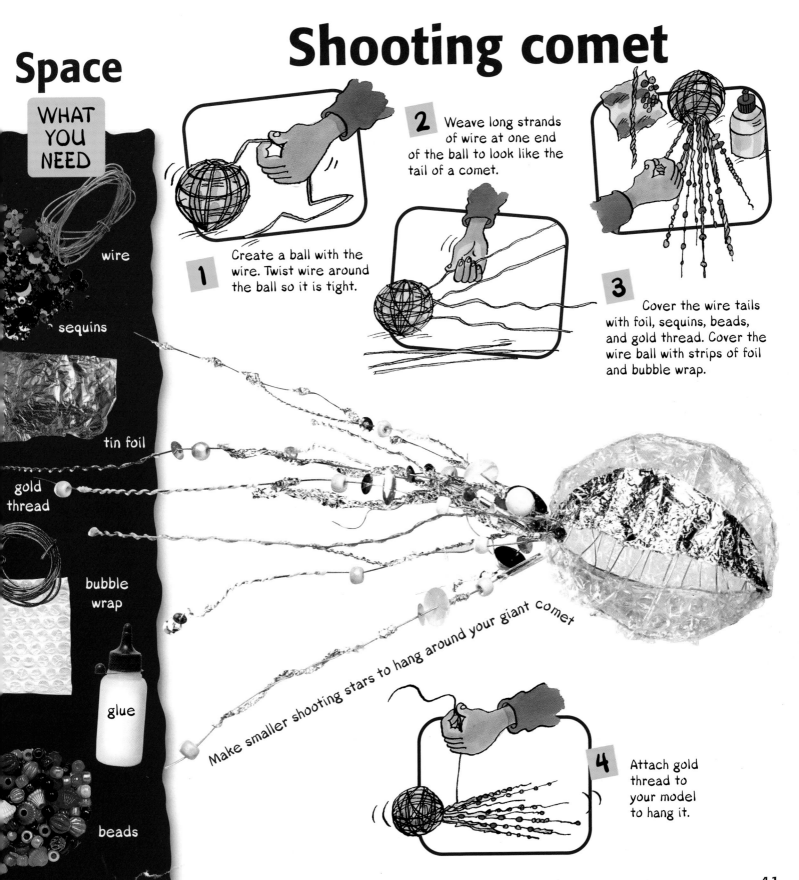

wire

sequins

tin foil

gold
thread

bubble
wrap

glue

beads

1 Create a ball with the wire. Twist wire around the ball so it is tight.

2 Weave long strands of wire at one end of the ball to look like the tail of a comet.

3 Cover the wire tails with foil, sequins, beads, and gold thread. Cover the wire ball with strips of foil and bubble wrap.

4 Attach gold thread to your model to hang it.

Make smaller shooting stars to hang around your giant comet

Black holes

Black holes are the most mysterious objects in the universe. They are like invisible monsters that swallow anything that comes too close, including big stars and whole groups of planets. Even light and time are trapped by the gravity of black holes.

Dead stars

A black hole is the darkest thing in the universe. It is a region of space that has such high gravity that nothing can escape from it. A black hole is black because it gives off no light at all. Even light cannot travel fast enough to escape a black hole's gravity. Black holes are what is left when a giant star explodes and collapses. If the center, or core, of the star is heavy enough, it is crushed by its own gravity and collapses into a tiny, single point. If anything comes close to the hole, it is dragged inside by the black hole's gravity and disappears from the universe forever.

Proof of existence

If a black hole is close to a star, the hole's gravity will pull gas from the star toward it. The gas will spiral around the hole, getting hotter as it is pulled into the hole and giving off X-rays. Scientists can detect these X-rays, and although a black hole itself cannot actually be seen, the X-rays are proof that it exists.

Superweights

Black holes come in different sizes. Some weigh the equivalent of about sixteen Suns, while others are massive, weighing billions of times more than the Sun. In 1997, a group of astronomers found evidence of an enormous black hole at the center of the **Milky Way** and there may be millions more black holes hiding among the stars. Not all black holes are big. Some black holes are no bigger than an atom, although they can still weigh billions of tons.

Space

WHAT YOU NEED

cardboard box with lid

glue

glitter

gold thread

paints and brush

tape

sequins

scissors

gold and silver poster board

Viewbox

1

Cut the end out of a large rectangular box, leaving the lid on the box. Make a small hole at the other end.

2

Paint the box black, inside and out. Decorate the outside with painted stars, sequins, and glitter.

3

Paint a glittery swirl on the inside of the box around the small hole. Glue a triangular glitter trail on the base, leading toward the far end.

4

Decorate the sides with sequins, splattered paint, and gold and silver planets.

5

Stick stars on the glitter trail, going from large to small. Cut out and decorate different planets. Hang them with gold thread and tape.

Tape the planets to the lid of the box, so they hang down.

Shine a flashlight through the back of your box to create a shining universe.

43

Aliens

Have you heard about mysterious visitors from outer space who visit Earth in flying saucers? Some people think they make crop designs in farmers' fields.

We call these visitors aliens, but has anyone ever seen one? Probably not. As far as we know, aliens are just characters in science fiction stories or in people's imaginations. This does not mean they do not exist. Some day, we may find other life forms in the universe.

Is there anybody out there?

If aliens exist, it is likely that they are quite different from us. They would only look like us if their planet was identical to Earth. All life forms on Earth are based on the chemical element known as carbon. Carbon-based life forms need water in order to develop. So, aliens that look like us would have to come from a planet where there is carbon and water.

Another Earth?

There are millions of stars in the universe. Some could be similar to our Sun, with planets in orbit around them. Life, as we know it on Earth, depends on water and oxygen and can only exist in temperatures that are neither too high, nor too low. If a planet was the same distance from its star as we are from our Sun, it might have similar temperatures and be able to support life.

Do you believe in aliens? Some people think they often visit Earth.

Space

Alien life forms!

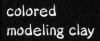

WHAT
YOU
NEED

colored
modeling clay

1

Break off pieces of clay
and roll them in your hands
to make them soft and
easy to model.

2

Form your own aliens with
funny and unusual bodies.

3

Roll thin sausage shapes
into arms and legs, spikes,
or even alien hairstyles!

4

Make tiny balls from
the clay and use them
for bumps, lumps, and
little green eyes.

Your alien can be
whatever you want it to
be - after all, who can
say you made it wrong?

You can also create weird alien plants by making colorful models with clay and wire

Glossary

asteroid A rocky object orbiting the Sun.

astronaut Someone who travels into space.

astronomers People who study the universe and everything in it.

atmosphere The layer of gas that surrounds a planet or star.

axis An imaginary line through the middle of a planet around which it spins.

black hole The collapsed center of a giant star, where the gravity is so strong that nothing can escape from it, not even light.

carbon dioxide A colorless, odorless gas made by humans and animals as they breathe out.

comet A giant lump of snow and dust that travels around the Sun. When it comes near the Sun, heat from the Sun causes it to release gas and dust, forming a tail.

constellations Patterns of stars in the sky. There are 88 known constellations.

fossils The remains of living organisms, preserved in rock.

galaxies Groups of billions of stars, held together by gravity.

gases Gases can flow, move easily, and expand into a larger space. The air we breathe is a gas.

giants (star) Very large stars, many times bigger than the Sun.

gravity A force that pulls objects toward each other. The bigger they are, or the closer they are, the stronger the pull of gravity.

habitable Some place suitable to live in or on.

helium One of the gases that a star is made from.

hydrogen The main gas in a star.

lens A curved piece of glass used to focus light.

lunar eclipse A darkening or hiding of all or some of the Moon as it passes into Earth's shadow.

magnet A force that attracts some materials to each other.

mass The amount of material in something.

matter The material – whether solid, liquid, or gas – that everything in the Universe is made from.

meteorite A piece of rock from space that lands on a planet or moon.

meteoroids Pieces of rock or dust in space.

meteors Bright streaks of light in the night sky, caused by pieces of rock or dust burning up in Earth's atmosphere.

Milky Way The galaxy to which the Sun and all the planets belong.

neutron star The remains of a collapsed star, made from matter compressed so much that it is made entirely from particles called neutrons.

nitrogen A colorless, odorless gas that occurs in the Earth's atmosphere.

nuclear energy Energy that can be released from the particles making up all matter.

observatories Places where people use telescopes to study space.

orbit The path taken by one object around another in space.

oxygen A colorless, odorless gas that is essential to plant and animal life.

pressure The strength of the force with which something presses.

protoplanets Large balls of rock, the original content of an asteroid.

quasars The very bright cores, or centers, of distant galaxies.

radio wave A form of energy that can travel through space and is invisible.

solar system The Sun and everything that orbits around it.

space probes Spacecraft sent to study a planet or space.

space station A spacecraft that orbits Earth, on which astronauts live.

star A large ball of gas in space that gives off light and heat.

supergiants (star) The biggest stars of all, up to 1,000 times bigger than the Sun.

supernova A massive star that has exploded, sending out clouds of dust and gas.

ultraviolet light An invisible type of light that is given off by very hot objects, such as the Sun.

white dwarf Dwarf stars are the smallest stars. A white dwarf is an old star.

X-rays An invisible form of energy similar to light.

Index

Materials guide

A list of materials, how to use them, and suitable alternatives

gold foil

silver foil

filler paste

PVA glue

flour

salt

cellophane or acetate

The crafts in this book require the use of materials and products that are easily purchased in craft stores. If you cannot locate some materials, you can substitute other materials with those we have listed here, or use your imagination to make the craft with what you have on hand.

Gold foil: can be found in craft stores. It is very delicate and sometimes tears.

Silver foil: can be found in craft stores. It is very delicate, soft and sometimes tears. For some crafts, tin or aluminum foil can be substituted. Aluminum foil is a less delicate material and makes a harder finished craft.

PVA glue: commonly called polyvinyl acetate. It is a modeling glue that creates a type of varnish when mixed with water. It is also used as a strong glue. In some crafts, other strong glues can be substituted, and used as an adhesive, but not as a varnish.

Filler paste: sometimes called plaster of Paris. It is a paste that hardens when it dries. It can be purchased at craft and hardware stores.

Paste: a paste of 1/2 cup flour, one tablespoon of salt and one cup of warm water can be made to paste strips of newspaper as in a papier mâché craft. Alternatively, wallpaper paste can be purchased and mixed as per directions on the package.

Cellophane: a clear or colored plastic material. Acetate can also be used in crafts that call for this material. Acetate is a clear, or colored, thin plastic that can be found in craft stores.

 1 2 3 4 5 6 7 8 9 0   Printed in the USA   0 9 8 7 6 5 4 3 2